GHOST HUNTER'S HANDBOOK

SUPERNATURAL EXPLORATIONS
FOR KIDS

LIZA GARDNER WALSH

Down East Books

Published by Down East Books
An imprint of Globe Pequot
Trade division of The Rowman & Littlefield Publishing Group, Inc.
4501 Forbes Boulevard, Suite 200, Lanham, Maryland 20706
www.rowman.com

Unit A, Whitacre Mews, 26-34 Stannary Street, London SE11 4AB, United Kingdom

Distributed by NATIONAL BOOK NETWORK

Designed by Lynda Chilton, Chilton Creative

British Library Cataloguing in Publication Information Available

Library of Congress Cataloging-in-Publication Data Available

ISBN 978-1-60893-570-3 (cloth : alk. paper)
ISBN 978-1-60893-571-0 (electronic)

♾™ The paper used in this publication meets the minimum requirements of American National Standard for Information Sciences—Permanence of Paper for Printed Library Materials, ANSI/NISO
Z39.48-1992.

To Bernie,
my favorite ghost
hunter.

TABLE of CONTENTS

INTRODUCTION

WARNING—READ AT YOUR OWN RISK!

D o you jump when you hear something go bump in the night and then quickly go to check it out? Instead of closing your eyes as you pass graveyards, do you actively explore them? Are you constantly asking questions that people don't have easy answers to? Have you ever seen an orb or a mist and tried to capture it on camera? Are you drawn to shows like *Ghost Hunter* or books like R.L. Stine's *Goosebumps*? If you answered yes to any of these questions, then my friend, you have the makings of a true ghost investigator. With all of those qualities working for you, you have a good head start. Kids also make some of the best ghost hunters because they tend to be more open-minded, have a sharp sixth sense (which means an ability to see things that aren't there), and ghosts trust kids more than grownups. Go figure!

I assume that since you picked up this book you believe in ghosts. This puts you with the 50% of Americans who believe in them. And maybe you can even count yourself among the 22% of people who have actually seen one.

I have always had an interest in ghosts. I lived in a haunted house growing up and constantly felt eyes on me. Now that I know more about ghost hunting, I know my childhood house would've been the perfect site for a hunt. It was a doctor's office and when people, um, perished, they were kept in our basement until they were buried. Yikes! Rather than try to pretend this wasn't happening, I eagerly embraced the spooky world that surrounded me. I spent hours in the graveyard, read local history, and took notes on the things I heard in the night. I also developed a real love for reading and telling a good ghost story. But I never really saw anything that I could definitely say was a ghost. So I remained skeptical but still very interested.

Fast forward twenty or so years to when I wrote a book about an old fort that was haunted. I finally got to experience what all the fuss was really about. I went on ghost hunts, spent most of a night in the fort with ghost hunters, and saw how they used all of their high-tech equipment. I heard footsteps, had a conversation with a ghost through a ghost box, and even felt a cold chill as I walked through one of the most haunted parts of the fort. But I still didn't see a ghost.

Then it happened. My daughter and I were walking through the fort on a regular old day when our flashlight suddenly blacked out. Something crossed in front of us, something black and shadowy. We gripped each other's hands tightly. Then a huge blast of smoke surrounded us. Without saying a word, we ran until we got to a part of the fort that was a lot less spooky—Outside.

Now I can say that I have indeed seen a ghost, or at least something like one. But even though I have had some experience, I still keep a

SOME KEY WORDS TO KNOW

PARANORMAL: Experiences that are very strange and cannot be easily explained by scientists.

ENTITY: A classification for any type of disembodied being, including a ghost, spirit, or poltergeist.

HAUNTING: Repeated appearances of spirits and ghosts.

APPARITION: The appearance of a paranormal being.

EMF: Electromagnetic Field. Varying degrees of electrical charges found in anything that relies on electricity or creates a magnetic field.

EVP: Electronic Voice Phenomena. Sounds that are not heard when they are spoken but only on recordings.

healthy dose of skepticism. As one of television's premier ghost hunters, Chris Gutcheon, said about one of his early sightings, "Was it a ghost? I don't know for sure. But I know I definitely saw something that I couldn't explain."

The question remains, does all of this make you excited and curious and want to know more? Tracking ghosts shouldn't be frightening, but it should definitely be fun. It can test your powers of observation and your ability to connect the dots. But the biggest thing of all is that ghost hunting is not necessarily about capturing ghosts or getting rid of them, but just trying to prove that ghosts actually exist. Most ghost hunters believe they are scientists using the scientific method. It is the job of a true ghost hunter to not only observe ghostly activity but to record it, and maybe even communicate with ghosts.

This book will help you do that. We will discuss the long history of ghosts, types of ghosts, where to find them, as well as different ways people come in contact with them. We will go through the skills and equipment needed to become a ghost hunter and how to go about an investigation. And once you've had some really spooky and mysterious encounters, we will talk about how to tell a really good ghost story. There is even a place to write down your observations and keep track of your sightings.

There will be time for a few words of caution later, but for now, arm yourself only with the power of curiosity and exploration. Seek to prove the unknown. As with any hobby or activity worth pursuing, you will need a healthy dose of patience. Not every house will produce eerie sounds and not every walk through the graveyard will bring ghostly

mists. But if you concentrate on collecting evidence and keep an open mind, who knows what waits for you in the ether. As Chris Gutcheon asks, "Are you ready? Can you set your fears aside and put your skills to the test? Are you prepared to do the research and take all the necessary precautions? And are you mentally prepared to run the risk of bumping into a real ghost?" Well, if so, then onward young ghost hunter!

GHOSTLY ENCOUNTER

"It was in the beginning of the school year and we were doing reading groups. We were allowed to spread out, so my group sat on the stairs going up to the middle school attic, which is called the Crow's Nest. We all saw this weird red light glowing from under the door and we kept seeing strange shadows."

~Mitchell

CHAPTER 1

HISTORY OF GHOSTS AND GHOST HUNTING

Throughout time, people have tried to make sense of ghosts and what happens after we pass on from life to the great beyond. Most ancient cultures had elaborate rituals to protect their communities from bad spirits, whether it was simply wearing a special amulet around the neck or painting pictures depicting the underworld. The general thought about ghosts in these cultures was that they were the restless spirits of the dead who hadn't finished up their earthly business. So most rituals were carried out to make sure that after someone died their business was 100% finished.

You probably know a bit about mummies and the elaborate events performed to ensure that the Egyptian dead had everything they needed. Egyptians believed in Ka, which is the spirit that lived inside the body, so when someone died, the Ka left the body. If priests did not perform special rituals to feed and nurture the Ka it could begin to haunt the living.

In ancient Egypt, offering tables like this, with drawings of food and drink, were left near tombs to give the spirit sustenance in the afterlife.

The earliest known ghost story comes from around 40 BC, when a philosopher known as Athenodorus rented a well-known haunted house in Athens, Greece. One night, Athenodorus heard the rattling of chains and saw a sad old man walking through the house and out to the garden. When he followed him outside, the old man had disappeared, but Athendorus was convinced he had seen something. The next day, he hired workers to come and dig in the garden, where they found a skeleton in rusty chains. When the bones were finally buried and resting in peace, the haunting stopped for good.

Ancient Greek and Roman cultures believed firmly in ghosts and the need for a restful spirit. Ancient Romans even created and celebrated a nine-day festival in May called *Lemuria*, which was dedicated to soothing the bad spirits, known as "lemures." These spirits apparently wandered through the night unable to find peace and were often the result of violent deaths. The hope was that after the spirits were soothed they would travel back to the underworld and cause no further damage.

The Dark Ages were a treasure trove of ghostly activity. Some people believed that witches and wizards had mysterious powers, and devils and demons haunted the peaceful nights. Huge numbers of people were killed through warfare, plagues, and witch hunts. All of this activity would certainly make for some pretty restless spirits. The ghost story, "The Ghost of Beaucaire," comes from this dark time. According to legend, the ghost was a young boy named William who was killed violently in a street fight. A week after his untimely death, William's spirit appeared to his eleven-year-old cousin, Marie. At first the young girl was scared, but she soon real-

A ghostly visitation

ized it was her cousin and that he was trying to tell her things. Soon William had shared secrets of life after death with his friends, family, and neighbors.

Throughout history, England has been a hotbed of paranormal activity. During the 1800s, people throughout England began to get very interested in seeing ghosts. Seances were held so people could talk to the dead. Ghost stories were told at parties held in haunted houses. All of this ghost fever began a movement called Spiritualism, which spread like wildfire and even traveled across the Atlantic Ocean to America. The rise of Spiritualism led to one of the biggest and most well-promoted ghost encounters in America.

Two teenage sisters named Kate and Margaret Fox began to witness some very strange and disturbing events. They heard periodic rapping on the walls of their house in Hydesville, New York. The sisters tried to talk to this spirit, naming him Mr. Splitfoot and asking specific questions, which they believed he answered correctly. Mr. Splitfoot told them things they claimed no one else could know. Soon the girls were traveling up and down the East Coast, performing in front of large audiences. Their demonstrations both fascinated and outraged the public, but as they shared their visions, Spiritualism took on a life of its own.

Kate and Margaret Fox

Later, a group of scientists in London started the Society for Psychical Research to get to the bottom of these mysterious reports and ghost sightings. This group took psychic research very seriously and wanted to study all manner of paranormal abilities and activities. This was the official birth of ghost hunting as a scientific endeavor to prove or disprove paranormal activity through the use of the scientific method. The Society is still active today.

HARRY HOUDINI

One of the most famous psychic investigators was Harry Houdini, the famous escape artist and magician. When his mother died in the 1920s, Houdini desperately sought a medium to contact his mother's spirit. A medium is a person who believes he or she can communicate with the dead. Instead of contact, he encountered only frauds, so he turned his energy to proving that

Harry Houdini

mediums were not only fake but were actually cheating people. Houdini made a pact with friends that if he could contact them from the afterlife, he would. So he made a code that he shared with his wife, Bess. After he died on Halloween, his wife desperately sought to contact his spirit, but no medium got close to unraveling the secret code. Still, each year, Bess held a seance to plead with Houdini's spirit to contact her. In 1936, she broadcast the seance on the radio and when nothing happened, she officially gave up, saying, "My last hope is gone. I do not believe Houdini can come back to me—or to anyone . . . it is finished. Good night, Harry." At that very moment, the sky opened up and a tremendous lightning storm began. The guests at the seance later learned that the storm was a microburst and occurred only over the radio station. Sounds like a pretty good magic trick, Houdini!

HARRY PRICE

Another well-known ghost hunter named Harry also dedicated much of his life to debunking fraudulent mediums and questioning supposed haunted houses. Harry Price was a member of the Psychical Society and was considered to be one of the first official ghost hunters. He had a wide audience since he often wrote about his encounters in the newspaper. The wide-range of modern equipment he acquired included such items as a thermograph, which monitors the temperature of a room and records it on graph paper. The impressive toolkit continued to grow throughout his career and shows the development and progression of modern ghost-hunting equipment.

Harry Price's ghost-hunting kit, which contained cameras for both still and moving pictures, tools for sealing doors and windows, apparatus for secret electrical controls, steel tape, drawing instruments, torch, bottle of mercury, and powdered graphite for finger-printing.

Oddly, as many homeowners renovate their older houses, they have found shoes buried deep in the walls of their houses. Oftentimes it is a child's shoe, sometimes a single ice skate. These shoes are known as "conceal-ment shoes," and were placed in the walls by Colonial Americans who believed they would ward off bad spirits.

GHOSTLY ENCOUNTER

"One time I saw a ball of white light. When I reached out to touch it, it was gone, but a chill started in my finger and went all the way through my body." ~Cooper

CHAPTER 2
TYPES OF GHOSTS AND HAUNTINGS

GHOST

1. The spirit of a dead person, especially one that is believed to appear to the living in bodily form or to haunt specific locations.

2. A person's spirit or soul.

3. A returning or eerie memory or image.

Every year on Halloween, kids with white sheets draped over their heads float from house to house to collect candy. This costume depicts the most classic idea of a ghost—a white, flowing image. But there are many other kinds of more elaborate ghosts. Spirits can take many shapes, including that of an orb or a fleeting black shadow, but often spirits look pretty similar to us. Certain spirits and hauntings, however, have been known to take some pretty unusual forms. There are reports of ghost cows, ships, cars, and even haunted swing sets.

TYPES OF GHOSTS

ORBS: Orbs are spherical balls of energy, not always visible with the naked eye but captured in photographs. Ghost hunter Dave Juliano defines an orb as, "the energy being transferred from a source (i.e., powerlines, heat energy, batteries, people, etc.) to the spirit so they can manifest. The spherical shape is the most energy efficient shape for a spirit to assume. There is a lot of controversy around the subject of orbs. Some ghost hunters dismiss them entirely. Many times orbs in a photo mean that there was dust on the lens or rain or snow falling, especially if there are lots of them. But if your photo shows just one orb that is fairly large in size with a slightly fuzzy edge, that usually means you have a genuine orb.

MISTS: Vaporous and nebulous masses that appear in photographs that often resemble smoke are considered mists. Mists sometimes form outlines of bodies or faces. Ghost hunter Joshua Warren says that "mists may be phantoms in a state of transition from one form to another." Ectoplasm, which came to fame in the movie *Ghostbusters*, can be considered a mist, even though it is a goo-like substance. Often people who see this report it as a swirling, glowing mass of mist.

GHOST LIGHTS: Mysterious lights that appear in the distance and have no known point of origin are called ghost lights. They are usually white or yellow and don't always appear consistently. The most famous ghost lights are called the Brown Mountain Lights of North Carolina. There is even a U.S. Geological Survey sign that alerts travelers: "The long, even-crested mountain in the distance is Brown Mountain. From early times, people have observed weird, wavering lights rise above this mountain, then dwindle and fade away." Legend has it that the lights began after a local woman disappeared. People said her husband killed her but he was never arrested. The lights stopped for several years but then a hiker found a skeleton of a young woman and the lights came back and have been sometimes seen in the night sky ever since.

SHADOW GHOSTS: Also known as shadow people, these ghosts are not human-like and have very few details other than a black shapeless form. The movements of this kind of spirit are said to be jiggly, abnormal, and even slippery.

RESIDUAL GHOSTS: A residual ghost does the same thing over and over again, such as making the same sound at the same time every day, or walking across a room at the same time. Some examples are sounds of children playing, a spirit that watches from a high hill or window, and a spirit that wanders the same path in a house. These ghosts are also known as energy remounts and memory imprints. The key thing about them is that they never interact with the people around them and they never do anything different. Think of it like a video recorder taking a movie of an event then playing it back over and over throughout time.

SPIRITS: are what most people imagine when thinking about a ghost. Spirits have unique and distinct personalities. They tend to be inter-active, leaving behind traces of evidence such as changing tempera-tures and smells. They are the ghosts that give you the feeling of being watched and occasionally they will go so far as to reach out to touch you. They are not especially bad or good and they don't follow the same routines the way residual ghosts do.

POLTERGEISTS: are the baddies of the spirit world—Trouble with a capital T. Most scary ghost movies are about poltergeists. Although they are rarely seen, these ghosts like to make themselves known. They will move things, slam doors, float furniture, and occasionally touch people. They can even produce very disgusting smells. Interestingly, these spirits are most often seen and felt by teenagers. Some ghost hunters believe that poltergeists are the by-product of turbulent teenage energy. If you ever feel that you have come in contact with a poltergeist, leave. Get a grownup, maybe even a ghost hunter, and do not continue messing with this energy. Heed the advice of the famous ghost hunters from the SyFy channel, who advise, "When in doubt, get the heck out."

ANIMAL GHOSTS: Many pets seem unwilling to leave their owners even after death, which leads to a lot of animal ghosts floating around. The most common and often seen animal ghosts are cats. Who knows, maybe with nine lives, they just get used to sticking around? According to author and researcher, Dusty

Rainbolt, there is a spirit cat who guards the Capitol Building in Washington, DC. This cat protects the ceremonial platform in the rotunda where dead presidents occasionally lie in state and is known to be quite ferocious.

Ghost dogs are often reported as well, and while some are the beloved family pet, some ghost dogs have a more demonic presence and appear with red eyes. The folklore of many nations holds that mischievous spirits often take the form of a black dog. But cats and dogs are not the only animal ghosts around. There have been sightings of horses, large groups of hounds, and even a herd of cows known as the Mesa Stampede Ghosts.

SIGNS YOU HAVE A GHOST

- Objects disappear then might reappear in very different places.
- Cold spots appear in otherwise well-heated, insulated rooms.
- You notice a sense that someone is watching.
- You hear strange sounds.
- Doors and windows open and close on their own.
- Lights, a radio, or the television turn on and off by themselves.
- Strange smells, with no known source, appear, such as cooking smells, perfume, tobacco smoke, flowers, or even the smell of the ocean.
- Your dog barks at the air or refuses to go in certain areas of the house.

GHOST OBJECTS: One of the most famous ghost objects is a ghost ship known as *The Flying Dutchman.* This story has been shared by sailors for more than one hundred and fifty years, and if you ever see it while sailing, it is not a good omen. The story goes that Dutch sea captain Hendrik VanderDecken was sailing around the Cape of Good Hope during a terrible storm. The captain was so determined to make record time that he refused to seek refuge or even take in the sails. One of the crew grabbed the wheel to try and steer toward shore but VanderDecken threw the man overboard. As they faced the fury of the storm, the captain swore with such fearful and awful curses that when he and his ship were indeed lost at sea, he was condemned to sail the seas for eternity for his negligence, the murder, and his terrible curses.

There is also a mysterious swing set in Argentina that residents have declared haunted. There is a video on YouTube that shows someone holding the swings very still and steady and then walking away. Before long, the swings begin to take off, rocking on their own as if there is an invisible child pumping his or her legs.

The Brown Lady

One of the most famous ghostly images ever caught on camera is that of the Brown Lady of Raynham Hall in Norfolk, England. This ghost image was captured by photographers in 1936 and published in *Country Life Magazine*. The image of the Brown Lady has been seen by many people and is said to be the ghost of Lady Dorothy Walpole.

Her story is quite sad, as she died a prisoner in her own home. Legend tells that her husband, Charles Townsend, was convinced she was in love with another man. In his jealous rage, he locked her inside their huge country estate and didn't allow her to see visitors or even her children. Her ghost appears dressed in a brown gown with a very sad expression on her pale face.

The ghost of Lady Dorothy Walpole

Famous Ghosts Throughout History

Anne Boleyn

Marie Antoinette

Abraham Lincoln

Dante

Napoleon

Nero

Harry Houdini

John Lennon

Robert E. Lee

Jesse James

Elvis Presley

Marilyn Monroe

Betsy Ross

WHAT ELSE COULD A GHOST BE OTHER THAN A GHOST?

Scientists all over the world are looking at ghostly phenomena and applying the scientific method. Many theories have emerged, but the investigation continues. Professor, Researcher, and Psychologist Richard Wiseman has conducted extensive research on the possible scientific explanations for what we think of as ghosts.

MAGNETISM: Some Canadian research-ers believe that at the bottom of most hauntings is a force called geomag-netism. This is when the movement of natural forces, such as solar flares and shifts in the earth's tectonic plates, cause strong magnetic fields. These sci-entists believe that these forces could also stimulate the part of the brain that causes hallucinations.

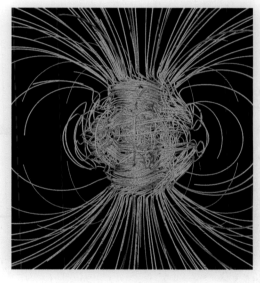

Atomic particles react to a magnetic field.

INFRASOUND: This theory poses that some of the creepy activities in haunted houses could be caused by low frequency sounds. Professor Vic Tandy came up with this theory after seeing a gray ghostly image in his workshop. The next day he noticed that his fencing sword was vibrating for no apparent reason. After several days of investigating, he determined it was all caused by a fan that was emitting a deep, low noise that human ears couldn't hear. Tandy showed that this infrasound caused the vibrations and may have even caused his eyeball to vibrate, making him see the gray optical illusion.

Is it a ghost caused by the power of suggestion, or just a trick of photography?

PSYCHOLOGICAL: Many scientists believe that people see ghosts because of what is called the power of suggestion. Just hearing that a house is haunted makes people more likely to report seeing a ghost in it.

TEMPERATURE: Many ghost hunters and paranormal investigators look at temperature changes as proof that there is ghostly activity. Researchers contest that old houses are often drafty due to poor insulation.

How to Protect Yourself Against Bad Stuff

To protect yourself from spirits who might not be the best to pal around with, there are a few established techniques.

- Picture a bubble of white light, like the one that Glinda the Good Witch of Oz appears in, and envision that bubble surrounding you and keeping anything out that is not good and light.

- Imagine you are a knight and are covered with big plates of metal armor.

- Find some kind of a lucky charm to bring with you on investigations. This is known as a sigil. Sigils are magical charms that form an energy barrier around you, and have been used for hundreds of years.

- Lighting a white candle is a good way to clear the energy after you have had a scary experience. Another trick is to buy a bundle of sage at your local health food store. Light this and let the smoke purify the area and clear out the energy. Remember to always have an adult nearby when you use matches.

- After any ghost experience, take a bath with Epsom salts.

- To keep ghosts away from your house, add wind chimes, plants, and sweep often to get the bad energy out. Another perk to this is that it will make your parents really happy.

If all else fails, you can chant this German charm to protect against nightmares: "I lay me down to sleep; No nightmare shall plague me until they swim all the waters of the earth and count all the stars in the sky."

Fort Knox in Maine, lit up to appear
especially spooky

GHOSTLY ENCOUNTER

" It was Halloween night and it was dark. We were driving down our road and we saw a transparent silhouette moving, kind of like a person but sort of dragging across the ground. " ~Finn

CHAPTER 3
FINDING GHOSTS

So now that we have covered a little bit about the types of ghosts out there and some of their defining features, how do you go about finding them? What are the best places to begin your hunt? Your house? Your school? The graveyard? The library?

Here is a quiz created by ghost hunter Chris Gutcheon to determine if the first place you should start is your very own house.

1. Do you hear strange noises, like footsteps, during the night or when no one else is home?

2. Does something seem to be scaring your dog or cat? Does your dog or cat refuse to go into a certain room, or does your dog sometimes bark at something that is not there?

3 Are there unexplained hot and cold spots in your house?

4 Do you sometimes feel like someone is watching you when you know no one is there?

5 Do lights or electrical appliances turn off and on by themselves?

6 Does your bed sometimes feel like it is shaking or moving a little?

7 Do you sometimes see, out of the corner of your eye, strange shadows that seem to be moving?

8 Do you sometimes feel an invisible hand touching your arm or the back of your neck?

9 Is there one room in the house that freaks you out, and whenever you go in it, do you get shivers up and down your spine?

10 Do things seem to mysteriously move from one place to another in the middle of the night?

If you answered yes to any of these, then I would say an investigation is in order. But if your house isn't haunted, what next? The local cemetery, perhaps? Ghosts don't really love spending time in cemeteries. Sure their bodies are buried there, but their spirits return to the places that had the

most impact on them. Maybe it is the house they lived in, the school they taught in, or the library where they worked. Ghosts also tend to go back to places where they have unfinished business, especially if something tragic happened to them suddenly.

One place to start as you look for a good haunt is your library or town historical society. Ask the historians if there are any famous ghost stories that they know about. Are there any ghost tours of your town? If so, take a tour and get to know the guides—they are always a wealth of knowledge. Ask your friends and their parents if they know any spooky spots or have stories from growing up in the area.

It might help to have the definition of a haunted house in mind. A haunted house is any house that seems to contain unusual and unexplainable activity. This activity can range from strange, sudden temperature drops; noises with no obvious source; strong feelings of sadness or fear; objects moving on their own; and actual apparitions. This definition leaves a lot of room for interpretation, so a lot of houses could possibly be haunted. Another good tip is that houses and buildings located near running water tend to be more haunted because water is believed to generate a faint magnetic energy that spirits can use to manifest. Also, there is a belief that lava, quartz, and granite attract more hauntings. That is why large buildings like castles and prisons, which are made of lots of rock, are often haunted. Another key to finding areas with high amounts of paranormal activity is to locate places where a lot of suffering, pain, fear, and desperation have taken place, such as prisons, hospitals, and mental hospitals. On the list of the most haunted places in America, you will find that most sites are large, often made of stone, and have had a lot of human activity—not always the happy kind.

The famous Alcatraz prison. Surely all that rock and water, and the suffering of inmates, must make for some serious ghost activity.

THE HAUNTED HOUSE HALL OF FAME

"All houses in which men have lived and died
Are haunted houses: Through the open doors
The harmless phantoms on their errands glide,
With feet that make no sounds upon the floors."

—Longfellow

The following haunted places can be found in all the books on ghosts and hauntings. I like to think that they have earned trophies for being the most haunted or have made it into the haunted house hall of fame. Either way, these stories have some pretty wild stuff going and have had enough witnesses to make them bonafide haunted house stories.

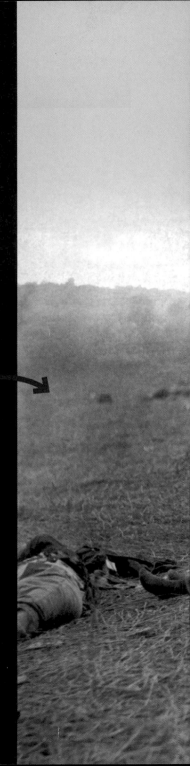

MOST HAUNTED SITES IN AMERICA

THE ALAMO
San Antonio, Texas

ALCATRAZ
San Francisco, California

BELCOURT CASTLE
Newport, Rhode Island

BELL WITCH CAVE
Adams, Tennessee

FORT KNOX
Prospect, Maine

GETTYSBURG BATTLEFIELD
Southern Pennsylvania

LEMP MANSION
St. Louis, Missouri

LINCOLN THEATER
Decatur, Illinois

MYRTLES PLANTATION
St. Francisville, Louisiana

WAVERLY HILLS SANATORIUM
Louisville, Kentucky

WINCHESTER MYSTERY HOUSE
San Jose, California

WINCHESTER MYSTERY HOUSE

William Winchester was treasurer of the Winchester Repeating Arms Company, which was founded by his father Oliver Winchester and was one of the earliest and most successful gun manufacturers. When he died suddenly of tuberculosis, William left a huge fortune to his young wife, Sarah. They had no children, so she was left with more money than she knew what to do with. After her husband's death, Sarah believed ghosts were following her everywhere. In her grief and fear, Sarah decided to consult a medium. The message that Sarah heard that day forever changed her life and caused her to create one of the weirdest houses in existence. The medium said that Sarah was indeed being haunted—by every single person who had been killed with a Winchester rifle.

With this prophecy in mind, Sarah headed to California, where she bought a modest house and began adding on to it. Construction started in 1884 and continued almost seven days a week until 1922. Sarah had her team of carpenters build stairways in cupboards and doors that could not be opened. The house was a giant maze meant to deter the spirits that followed Sarah day after day. By the time Sarah died, the Winchester Mansion had 160 different rooms and 40 of those were bedrooms. Many rooms were demolished as the work went on, but if all the original rooms remained, the mansion would have more than 350 rooms. Sarah renovated more than six hundred times. But the questions remain: was she trying to outrun the spirits or make a house that would hold them all, maybe even trap them? Why would one person need such a big house?

BORLEY RECTORY

Tucked deep in the English countryside, about an hour from the bustle of London, there once stood a sprawling red brick rectory known to be one of the world's most famous haunted houses. Built in 1863 by Reverend Henry Bull for his family, the rectory was a rambling place with thirty-five rooms. But very soon after it was built, strange things began to occur. Mysterious shadowy figures walked the gardens and loud noises cried out through the quiet country nights. There were even reports of writing that appeared on walls and the sound of shuffling feet throughout the building. Another often reported sound was of a coach rattling down the lane next to the house. For many years, inhabitants reported seeing a variety of ghosts at the rectory, but the most common sighting was of a nun. In one startling sighting, four of Henry Bull's daughters were return-ing from a garden party when they saw a woman in a black nun's habit

gliding across the lawn. When one of the women went to talk to the nun, the apparition disappeared suddenly.

Some historians claim the spot was once the site of a convent from the 1200s. Legends tell of a young nun who fell in love with a stagecoach driver. When they tried to run away and get married, she was found and sealed up alive in the wall of the convent to die a slow, painful death.

In 1939, a fire burned the building, leaving only a brick shell. People reported seeing strange figures that rose up out of the smoke and even the image of a nun standing in an upstairs window while flames roared below.

CHILLINGHAM CASTLE

This English castle near the Scottish border is said to be one of the world's most haunted castles. Perhaps it is due to the fact that people have lived within its walls for more than eight centuries, making it one of the most continually inhabited castles in England. Several distinct ghosts circle the halls of Chillingham, each with its own very distinct way of haunting.

THE BLUE BOY For some reason, this ghost always began its haunts at exactly midnight, when a loud and persistent wail would permeate the thick castle walls. These terrible moans were replaced by a glowing blue light around a particular four-poster bed, where a small, childish figure would then appear. In the 1920s this room and areas nearby were renovated, and when the floor was dug up, workers found the bones of a young boy surrounded by fragments of blue cloth. After the bones were buried, the ghost of the Blue Boy was never seen or heard again.

LADY MARY BERKELEY A spirit that still roams the grounds of Chillingham is Lady Mary Berkeley, whose husband, the Earl of Tankerville, left her alone in the castle and ran off with her sister. She often walks around the border of the property looking for him. People have even reported seeing her apparition step out of her portrait, which hangs in the nursery.

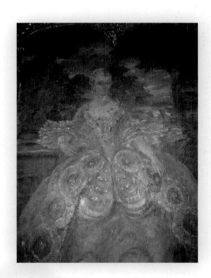

STIRLING CASTLE

Although this castle was the site of the coronation of Mary, Queen of Scots, it was also witness to horrific battles and great tragedies. Several ghosts continue to haunt the castle, including the Green Lady and the Pink Lady.

THE GREEN LADY This apparition is thought to be a loyal servant of Mary, Queen of Scots. Legend says that she had a vision that the queen was going to be engulfed in flames. When she ran in to the queen's chambers, there was indeed a fire, and although the queen was spared, the maid perished. When this spirit appears, everyone at the castle knows to look out for danger.

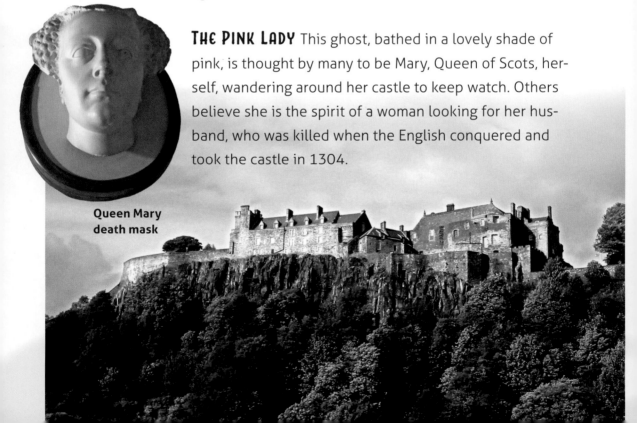

THE PINK LADY This ghost, bathed in a lovely shade of pink, is thought by many to be Mary, Queen of Scots, herself, wandering around her castle to keep watch. Others believe she is the spirit of a woman looking for her husband, who was killed when the English conquered and took the castle in 1304.

Queen Mary death mask

THE HOUSE OF FACES

One of the eeriest and most fascinating haunted houses is in a tiny town in Spain called Belmez de la Moraleda. One day, a woman named Maria Pereira was cleaning her kitchen when she noticed a mark on her floor. She scrubbed it but it wouldn't go away. Over the next few days, the mark got even more defined and began to take the shape of a face. No matter how hard they scrubbed, the family could not get rid of it.

After much frustration and confusion, Maria's son Miguel took a sledgehammer and destroyed the area in order to lay a new floor. As soon as the new floor had dried, a face appeared again almost immediately. They repeated the process of putting a new floor down, but still the face appeared. Soon more faces began to emerge. One was of a woman with her hair flying in all directions. Sometimes small crosses appeared. Many people throughout the town and region witnessed this startling event and no one could find an explanation. Finally, the family agreed to have the area excavated and human remains were uncovered, including two headless skeletons. Locals from the village recalled that the street where this house was located had been built on top of an old cemetery.

At one point, Professor de Argumosa, who spent much time study-ing these apparitions, set up a voice recorder. When it was played back, cries were heard as well as words, such as "spirits, drunkard, little grand-child." The mystery of the House of Faces was never solved and despite the uncovering of the skeletons, the faces continue to appear, making this house a tourist attraction and a supernatural marvel.

GHOSTLY ENCOUNTER

"Me and my mom were in Fort Knox in this long hallway where the steps go up and then down. There was all of this dripping water and then suddenly the air got really cold around us and we started to run." ~Ava

CHAPTER 4
HOW TO BE A GOOD GHOST HUNTER

To be a good ghost hunter doesn't necessarily mean that you have seen the most ghosts or have the fanciest ghost-tracking equipment. It especially doesn't mean you have to watch hours of ghost hunting shows on television. The number-one quality of a ghost hunter is similar to those that birdwatchers and fossil hunters share—good observation skills, otherwise known as the ability to pay attention. This kind of paying attention is not like in school. This is the extra-sensory kind of attention, meaning all of your senses are alert—ears, eyes, gut, and the eyes in the back of your head. Some other traits include patience, courage, and knowing how to be objective about things, which means not letting your feelings cloud your judgment. Another invaluable skill is to listen to what your gut is telling you so that you can always make safe and sound decisions. All in all, ghost hunters need to pay attention, record what they see, and then make conclusions.

Working in this field is a little like what you do in science class. You are looking for proof. The challenge is that scientists haven't found definite proof that ghosts are real because ghosts are difficult to study. Science is about observation and measurement, but ghosts are anything but predictable and you can't just grab one and weigh it! It is also impossible to know exactly when to look. Some hunts are super productive and filled with research, while others provide nothing but a lot of garbled noises and false alarms. So all you can do is keep an open mind and continue to collect clues and information.

Even if you believe with all of your heart that ghosts are real, even if you have seen ghosts, orbs, or strange things move, or felt the hairs on the back of your neck stand up, there is always the need as a ghost hunter to remain slightly skeptical. That means to always keep in mind the possibility that ghosts might not be real. The following advice from established ghost hunters helps with this idea. According to ghost hunter Grant Wilson, "If you set out to prove a haunting, anything will seem like evidence. If you set out to disprove it, you'll end up with only those things you can't explain away." Lori Summers states, "You might think a ghost hunter tries to capture ghosts, or eliminate them, or drive them away. But what most ghost hunters are hunting aren't ghosts, precisely, but real, concrete evidence that ghosts exist." Basically, don't jump to conclusions, because many of the cases that seem the most indisputable often can be explained as natural occurences.

Chris Gutcheon describes what he calls the the three Es of ghost hunting: evidence, equipment, and exploration. "Evidence is the what, equipment is the how, and exploration is the where." Soon we will discuss

WHAT DO YOU SAY TO A GHOST?

It might be an awkward moment if you actually meet a ghost but don't know what to say. You might even feel a bit tongue-tied, and you certainly can't ask, "How's the weather?" Here are some ideas from ghost hunter Lori Summers:

- How long have you lived here?
- Where are you from?
- Do you know what year it is?
- Do you live here, or are you just visiting?
- Why are you here?
- Do you have a message for us?

QUOTE FROM A YOUNG GHOST HUNTER

Ever since I was little I believed in ghosts. I watched ghost shows with my father, and when I was old enough he brought me with him on hunts. I like to adventure into the unknown and process unexplained things in my mind. Paranormal experiences are reported every day, and as time moves forward we are getting closer to the answers.

To be a good ghost hunter you need to be dedicated and patient. You need the right mindset; a person needs to keep an open mind to all possibilities. Science is a major factor in ghost hunting to understanding the different forms of energy and how they function in the paranormal world. Every ghost hunter also should be spiritually grounded so he or she can understand the difference between positive and negative energies.

~Bryanna

what equipment you need to get started so that you can begin your explorations and gather your evidence. But it is important to know what to look for. The two main types of evidence that ghost hunter's depend on are EVPs and EMFs. EVPs are unexplained audio events that are not detected by the ear but are picked up by recording devices and are not heard until played back after the hunt is over. This technique was discovered in the 1950s when a bird watcher was recording bird songs. When he listened to his tape, in addition to bird songs, he heard lots of strange human voices. EMF recordings note when there is a charge of electromagnetic energy. The theory is that ghosts use electromagnetic energy to take form. False readings on an EMF detector are often picked up if a microwave is nearby, cell phones are being used, or radios, air conditioners, or TVs are within one hundred yards. Temperature changes, noises you can hear, as well as actual sightings are also important forms of evidence.

EQUIPMENT NEEDED FOR A GHOST HUNT

When starting out with this hobby, it is tempting to spend a lot of money on gadgets. But all you really need to get started is a flashlight, a compass, something to record voices or EVPs, and a decent camera.

The compass is perhaps the most dependable and often forgotten piece of equipment in the ghost hunter's toolkit because it is a very reliable electromagnetic field sensor. You must have a good flashlight,

and, if you want to go an extra step, you can even add a red filter, which will help keep your eyes adjusted to the dark. You also need to wear the right clothing. If you are going to do an investigation outside or in a cold place, it is a good idea to wear layers and comfortable clothing. Ghost hunters often wear clothing with lots of pockets to carry their gear, pens, flashlights, and phones. The following list gives a good sense of what you need for a hunt if you are really going to make this hobby a part of your life.

There's an App for That

If you have access to a smartphone, there is a fun app called Ghost Radar, which uses a kind of radar screen to alert you to nearby ghosts. The ghosts appear as a ball of either green, red, or yellow light depending on how close they are, and the screen lets you see whether they're behind you, in front, or off to one side. You will also hear words as the ghosts try to communicate. Who knows how accurate it is, or if it's even real, but it's a fun way to turn a get together with friends into a ghost hunt.

BASICS

- × Compass: If the needle is not pointing due north or if it spins, then a powerful magnetic field is affecting it. A compass can also help you keep from getting lost if you're ghost hunting in a large area outside.

- × Flashlights and head lamp

- × Notebook and pens

- × Watch

- × Extra batteries

- × Food and water

- × Cell phone (turned off so as not to interrupt the EMF detectors)

- × Walkie-talkies (if you are with a group)

GHOST-HUNTING DEVICES

THERMOMETER: Detects cold spots where a ghost may be located. Ghost hunters prefer remote sensor wireless thermometers.

ELECTRONIC FIELD METER OR K2 SENSOR: Picks up electromagnetic activity.

VIDEO CAMERA

DIGITAL CAMERA: Remove infrared and ultraviolet settings to take a full-spectrum image.

INFRARED METER: To detect sources of heat.

A thermograph creates a chart of temperature changes.

AUDIO ENHANCER: A device that enhances low sounds.

NIGHT VISION SCOPE: Allows a hunter to see in the dark.

SPIRIT BOX OR GHOST BOX: A tool that searches AM radio bands to find white noise for the ghost to speak through.

OVILUS PX: A dictionary box that allows the ghost to speak, searching through over 2,000 word choices.

THE GHOST-HUNTING TEAM

There are many ghost-hunting organizations throughout the country that do this activity as a hobby. Most groups do not get paid to be ghost hunters and only do it because they are interested in uncovering the mysteries surrounding paranormal activities. The following is a list of some of the "jobs" that people have in these organizations.

EVP SPECIALIST: Focuses on recording sounds that are also known as electronic voice phenomena.

INVESTIGATOR: Actively searches for evidence using a variety of equipment.

SENSITIVE/PSYCHIC: Claims to see spirits and other paranormal presences.

RESEARCHER: Looks for historical information to back up haunting evidence.

TECH TEAM MEMBER: Troubleshoots equipment, backs things up to computers, and downloads EVPs and video to computers. Makes sure all of the equipment is operating without problems.

GHOST PHOTOGRAPHS

These are the images that ghost hunters hope will show up on their computer after an investigation. Orbs can often just be dust in the air or on the lens, but are still something to look closely at. Although there are some special cameras and settings that can help to capture ghostly images, a pretty good digital camera should work to start with. K and

L Soul Searchers recommends that you always have a few people look at your photos because often someone will pick up something that you missed on the first look. The prize is a bodied apparition—a ghost that actually appears in vaguely human shape, and ghost hunters are always on the lookout for these. Who knows, maybe you will capture one to enter into the archives of ghostly evidence. Bodied apparitions are very rare but are the most exciting finds for a paranormal investigator. One of the most famous is the Brown Lady of Raynham Hall.

As mentioned earlier in the section on types of ghosts, orbs are not seen with the eye but only captured in photos. Some ghost hunter's debunk orbs because they can often just be dust reflected by a flash. But if the orb has a fuzzy side and maybe is a different color than white, it often makes the ghost hunter look twice. Mists, as mentioned earlier also, are vaporous and nebulous masses that appear in photographs. Mists may form vague out-lines of bodies or faces and often have a smoky look to them.

NO OUIJA

Although you can buy a ouija board at almost every big toy store, most ghost hunters will steer you away from using one and insist that it is not in any way a toy. Using a ouija board, also known as a spirit board, is said to open the door to poltergeists and low-level psychic phenomena, a door that once opened is not easily shut. According to the article, "Ouija, Not a Game," author Dale Kaczmarek says that "spirits from the lower astral plane are most often attracted by these divination tools, and they introduce chaotic and sometimes dangerous energy into the homes of the naive." So even though it is tempting and seems like an innocent fun game, steer clear of the ouija!

GHOST HUNTER'S CODE OF CONDUCT

Like any good hobby, ghost hunting has a creed and an expectation of how people should act while on investigations. It is important to follow this code of conduct, no matter how big or small your investigation may be.

1 Always have a buddy with you and make sure a grownup is with you. Also have a phone on you in case you get separated.

2 Safety first. Check the site in the daylight before an investigation to plan the safest route and check for hazards.

3 Never trespass and always get permission from the owner before entering a haunted site.

4 Always wear proper clothing and have the right equipment.

5 If something gets too scary, leave the site immediately.

6 Always respect the ghosts and speak to them in a kind and steady manner.

7 Never break anything or damage property in any way.

8 Question everything and use careful research to determine what was uncovered.

TYPES OF PSYCHIC ABILITIES

Some people are born with an ability to see things that perhaps not everyone else can see. Maybe you know someone who has a better sense of how to stay out of trouble then the rest of the class—always sensing the teacher's return from the copy room before everyone else. Or maybe you have a friend who you are so connected to that you call each other at the exact same time. Some people might just be born with the ability to see ghosts, while others miss the creepy undertones. Even if you aren't able to read your mom's mind or predict what your teacher is going to give for homework, it doesn't mean that you won't be a good ghost hunter. Many of the following psychic skills can be developed with practice and all of them begin with the most important skill of all, paying attention and listening to the signals that your body gives you.

CLAIRSENTIENCE: Psychic feeling, often a feeling in your gut, a hunch, hairs on your neck standing up.

CLAIRCOGNIZANCE: Psychic knowing, following your intuition, simply knowing something is taking place.

CLAIRVOYANCE: Psychic seeing, as if you can see a scene in your mind like you are watching a movie.

CLAIRAUDIENCE: Psychic hearing, the ability to hear voices inside your head that others cannot.

QUESTIONS TO ASK BEFORE STARTING AN INVESTIGATION

- Was a seance held or a ouija board used?

- Are there any unexplained things—objects that move, noises?

- Do your pets refuse to go in certain areas?

- Did anyone ever die in the house that you know of?

- Do you know any of the history of the house?

- Has anyone been having bad dreams frequently?

The East Coast Ghost Trackers

> **"If immortality be untrue, it matter little whether anything else be true or not."**
>
> **–H.T. Buckle**

For the past several years on blustery autumn nights, The East Coast Ghost Trackers gather at Fort Knox in Maine for a ghost hunt. Clad in camouflage pants, black shirts, and tactical vests, they set up their command center for the throngs of people signed up to partake in their guided ghost hunts. Their vests are filled with valuable ghost-hunting equipment—EMF meters, which detect electro-magnetic fields; full-spectrum cameras; laser flashlights that set green webbed traps for ghosts to walk through; and various ghost boxes that ride the radio bands searching for the white noise that allow ghosts to communicate.

The excitement and eagerness is palpable as the group prepares for the evening's adventure. Early guests filter in, unsure of what to expect—some have seen ghosts before, some are looking for a ghost story to share at the bar later that evening, and some are desperate for a connection with a spirit to confirm their growing sense of extra-

sensory-perception. It is this building energy that co-founder Jamie Dube relies on as he takes his place as leader of the hunt. According to Dube:

> There is a lot that goes on when conducting a ghost tour. A lot of getting paranormal results/evidence is what I like to call "energy manipulation." I'm somewhat of a conductor with the energy and entities. On a ghost tour I place people in certain spots. Even my spot is crucial. Spirits are attracted to certain energy vibrations and auras. I make it easier for them to want to cooperate. I get everyone focused and placed. On tours, everyone has a different level of energy, and I have to balance it so the entities can communicate. I also try to get everyone to let go of any negative feelings or doubts before I start. One downer in the group can ruin the whole tour. I'm strict on a ghost tour because of this and very quick to keep the focus. Once I get all this leveled off then it's all about trust and coop- eration on the entity's part. Not all entities are nice, but the spirits at Fort Knox are content, it seems, for now, and eager for the contact. It's definitely a lot deeper than most know.

This intensity of energy belies the need for patience in pursuing spirits. For not every ghost hunt turns up para- normal activity. Still, the ghost hunters are determined to document the layers of evidence they've accumulated over the years. Most of the significant material they have uncov- ered is a direct result of hundreds of hours of investigation, and with each tour more evidence stacks up to confirm the haunted nature of the fort. They know the ins and outs of the fort and the various "hot spots," moving directly to those areas without wasting any time. Ken Ort and Jamie Dube

are the founders of the East Coast Ghost Trackers, and they have established a rapport with several of the entities that call the fort home and in so doing have determined that it is an intelligent haunt, one with distinct reactions that change depending on the group or the mood of the spirit. The group members consider themselves scientists seeking to prove there is life after death, and the fort is their laboratory.

Once Jamie has determined who will wield the instruments, gone over the fort rules, and warned of the abundance of bats, he and the other ghost hunters lead the group along the pebbled path into the fort. A few of the guests giggle nervously in the crowd, others clutch their partners, every one huddles under warm layers of clothing, and no one knows what to expect. The fort is maze-like in the daytime, but at night all sense of borders are blurred and even if you are sure of where you entered, in no time you feel completely turned around.

The tours always start in a spot where a spirit known as "Mike" haunts. As we approach a wider area, we are "placed" by Jamie, filling empty spaces and creating a web of bodies. Jamie pulls out his ghost box and asks Mike if he is here with us tonight. The static of the radio is jarring in this echo chamber and everyone cranes forward to listen as the radio attempts to detect a voice. "Mike, are you are here with us? Finish my count, one, two..." and the waves of radio fluctuate until a clear word rings out, "apple." It seems Mike is a trickster and delights in provoking Jamie because as the interactions with Mike continue and Jamie asks, "What do you want us to do?" a clear voice emerges from the ghost box and says, "scram." Mike has said people's names through the ghost box on other ghost hunts. Jamie reports that Mike prefers him to sit down, sometimes he obeys and sometimes he doesn't. But when he does sit, he can then usually get Mike to cooperate.

We follow Jamie back into the alleyway and line the sides. The brick is uneven in parts of this section and flashlights are needed, even as the apertures cut high in the granite walls let in tiny shimmers of moonlight. All of the people who have received EMF and K2 meters are called to the top of the alley where they hold their equipment up like magic wands. Some of the units are flashing green, but red means the electromagnetic field of a spirit has been detected. The goal is for the benign green lights to turn crimson. Jamie commands again, "go to red, on the count of three," we wait, the suspense building as a cold breeze slides down the alley. One of the ghost hunters stationed next to me whispers that the breeze is a ghost. Ghost hunters refer to this as "an ionic breeze," when a ghost gathers particles to form a coldness that acts as wind. Just as Jamie says we are leaving since nothing is happening, all three lights immediately turn from green to red. The crowd sighs collectively. Jamie says that tonight Mike is really playing with him, but somehow, it happened, the sensors were tripped.

Jamie leads us up a set of stairs into another area. The ghost trackers believe this area is home to an unintelligent haunt, a residual energy trapped in time. Last year they caught on infrared video a bar of light rising out of the floor and then moving from one wall to the other. The group theorizes that the imprinted energy is a remnant of something that happened in this area and is now trapped.

There is one paranormally charged alleyway in which a certain apparition often appears. Jamie says that this figure is "strong as heck, powerful, and wants to be respected." It is this same entity that they saw standing on top of the fort looking down at them one night after a long ghost hunt. On other hunts, people have been "touched" in this area, hats knocked off, hair pulled, pant legs tugged, and cold air blown on the backs of their neck. On one tour, a woman standing in an archway screamed as she felt this touch. Interestingly, it is mostly women who are touched at the fort.

The premiere stop on a ghost hunt at the fort is the Officers' Quarters. More paranormal experiences have occurred here than anywhere else. The old, pine planked floor creaks but that is not the only sound that is creepy, this area is where the ECGT have acquired most of their significant VPs—Voice Phenomena. Laughter, screams, and even what sounded like a cat shrieking, have all been recorded in this area. Ghost tours have often heard footsteps in the upstairs quarters and on a recent tour, the footsteps sounded like they were walking among the group.

Poltergeist activity, which occurs when an entity moves an object, is common in this part of the fort. People have heard something that sounded like a rock being thrown above them, hitting the floor and then rolling. Heavier things have thumped, like the sound of a trunk dropping. One time Jamie asked a spirit to move a wooden box and a half dozen people saw it shift. But people have also been touched in the Officers' Quarters. A teenager named Molly once felt something grab her elbow and pull her back into the room as she was trying to leave. She assumed it was her mother, but her mother wasn't near her. Amanda McDonald, a member of the

East Coast Ghost Trackers and an employee at the fort, always gets a strong whiff of pipe tobacco when she enters this area. But perhaps the most profound contact the group has made was during the first ever Halloween night ghost investigation at the fort, when the veil between worlds is the thinnest. More than thirty people witnessed the powerful ghost activity. The following from Jamie describes what occurred that night in the Officers' Quarters.

It was just after midnight and the room was full. The K2 meters were dead, not doing a thing. I tried to bring out the cloaked man and was not having any luck. I then switched gears and decided to call on the children at the fort. The moment I started asking for the kids to come and play, the K2 meters started going crazy. I then asked the little girl entity if her name started with the letter B. The K2 started going crazy. I then asked her if her name started with the letter E. Again the K2 meter was going crazy. I then started calling her Elizabeth and started working with her name. I asked her if she was five years old to light the lights up five times in a row for me. She did and more than once! I asked her if she had her mommy with her. My dictionary device said "Mom."

I asked her if her mom would help her move something in the room for us. The device said "mommy." I asked Elizabeth if she would go over and give someone a hug. A women from the group cried out in the pitch black, "Something is hugging me." Then another woman said, "Someone is holding my hand." I asked Elizabeth to make a noise so that we could hear her. We then heard voices from upstairs. It was a very interesting night and amazing to hit on the name Elizabeth. I think in time I will find out who these people are and maybe help them move on if they want.

INTERVIEW WITH K AND L SOUL SEARCHERS

K and L Soul Searchers is a small group of investigators who enjoy finding answers to the countless questions involved in the spirit world. They offer a popular class on ghost hunting and have led groups into some renowned haunts. They have offered confidential investigations for nine years and are committed to giving moral and spiritual support to those in need. The group co-founders have been to places such as Trans Alleghany Lunatic Asylum, The Mill Agent House, and Waverly Hills Sanitorium. I sat down with the founders, husband and wife Lee and Karen Bisson, to talk about their experiences.

When Lee Bisson was young, he and his brother were running laps around their childhood home. All of his family was sitting outside. When he got near the kitchen window, Lee saw an older woman standing in the window and heard a voice that said, "Run, Lee, run." He ran and for the first time ever he beat his brother in their race. When he told his mother what he had seen, she said that sounded like the ghost of his grandmother who had passed away before he was born. From that moment on, Lee began searching for ghosts and wondering why some spirits hung around on Earth. It started a lifelong quest to understand.

Karen never believed in ghosts until she met her husband and he dared her to go to Waverly Hills Sanatorium in Kentucky. After that trip she believed in ghosts 100 percent! Between the two of them, they have had some fun and very spooky adventures. They have heard ghost horses as if they were right next to them, caught shadow people on film, seen ghost children looking out windows at them, felt breathing on their neck, been chased by a black mist, and that is only the tip of the iceberg!

After so many investigations, the couple has lots of advice to share about what to do and not to do when ghost hunting:

✖ The most important thing is to be respectful. Never antagonize or talk down to spirits. Always talk to them in a nice, kind voice. Their motto is "Ghosts have feelings too."

✖ Always be with an adult who knows the place you are investigating and knows that it is filled with kinder ghosts and is a safe place to investigate.

✖ When you go into a place that is haunted, don't have any fearful or negative thoughts. Envision yourself surrounded by a white light and say at different times throughout, "I am safe, nothing can harm me."

✖ Don't over research before you go to a site because you might convince yourself of things and have certain expectations.

✖ Don't get discouraged. Sometimes you can go into a place and find nothing and then go back an hour later and have lots of things happen. The timing is very unpredictable.

✖ Always have someone else go through pictures and evidence with you just in case your eyes missed something.

✘ Get a good night's sleep before a ghost adventure. Ghosts take your energy to try and manifest and it can really drain you.

✘ Always put your hair up or wear a hat because some ghosts like to pull on your hair.

✘ Remember that many ghosts are just trying to get your attention and some of them can be a lot of fun. But you need to be very careful. and if you ever feel anything too scary, trust your instincts, grab your grownup, and run.

A ghostly shadow can be seen in the lower left of the window.

Telling ghost stories has been a pastime for generations.

GHOSTLY ENCOUNTER

"One time, when I was in Quebec, we were in this really old building and a terrible smell appeared out of nowhere."

~Bennett

CHAPTER 5
HOW TO TELL A GOOD GHOST STORY

What could be better than sitting around a fire with some of your good friends trying your best to scare the living daylights out of each other? Having a few good scary stories in your repertoire is a great way to keep a party lively. And to be a good storyteller, you have to know your audience. As with any ghostly activities, there is what I like to call the "fear-o-meter." Some of your friends might be 100 percent comfortable with getting spooked while others might have nightmares. It is always a good idea to gauge your friends' reactions on the fear-o-meter as the night of ghost stories progresses. I often have kids use their hand as if it is a dial to show where they fall on the scale between terrified and not scared at all. And I always remind people that at any time, they are free to leave and go back to their perfectly boring, unscary books. Just kidding.

The first step in telling a ghost story is to choose a really scary time to tell it. Here are what some kids I know suggested for setting the stage. Tessa suggested telling stories during a power outage by candlelight. Finn mentioned having friends come to a creepy place like an attic. Ava said that sleepovers late at night are perfect for ghost story telling.

Once you have the when, you can focus on the how: how to tell your story to give it the creepiest effect. Obviously, when telling your story you don't want to try to sound overly happy like you are reading a nursery rhyme. Instead, you can "sound like a creepy dead guy," as Mitchell suggested. Basically, the idea is to talk more quietly than you normally do

Every culture has ghosts and ghost stories. This 1899 illustration is from Japan.

so everyone has to lean in and listen harder. You also want to pause to let the tension build while providing some good asides, like, "You wouldn't know this, but five years before there was an attack in this house by Big Foot." The tone should be rather matter-of-fact so that the audience trusts you and will believe the story you are telling. To add to the creep factor, put a flashlight under your chin while you tell the story.

There are countless ghost story books at the library that recount some of the classics guaranteed to give a fright. Reading a few of these is a good way to start learning about what makes a good scary story and what they have in common. There are several stories that follow a formula but can be changed depending on location or age of the audience. One traditional story told around campfires is about a ghost hitchhiker. This tale is told in many different parts of the country, but usually the story takes place on a dark and foggy night where someone is hitchhiking late at night. The hitchhiker can be a kid, a bride, or an old man. The car slows down to offer the traveler a ride but when they arrive at the destination, the hitchhiker is no longer in the car. The following is a version of the hitchhiker story that is a little different and adds an even creepier twist. It is from *The Kids Campfire Books.*

We were driving along past the cemetery on a dark night not long ago. The rain was coming down in sheets. Suddenly I called out "Stop" to Mom. In our headlights I could see a boy on the side of the road. He was wearing only a T-shirt and shorts.

We stopped and he got into the back seat. He didn't talk much, but I remember he said his name was Jack. I soon noticed he was shivering and wet, so I offered him my sweatshirt.

He asked us to stop at the end of a driveway and he jumped out. When he got to the front door of his house, we drove off. It wasn't until later that I remembered he still had on my sweatshirt.

The next day, we had to drive down the same road to town, so Mom stopped at the house. We walked up to the door and knocked. An old man and woman answered and Mom told about offering Jack a ride in the rain and about the sweatshirt.

The old man said there had to be some mistake. Their son had been called Jack, but he died twenty-five years ago the night before. He was buried in the local cemetery.

When we got to town, Mom was doing the shopping so I walked to the cemetery and looked for his grave.

When I found Jack's headstone, lying on the ground in front of it was my sweatshirt, covered in leaves and soil.

If that doesn't give you a pit in your stomach, I am not sure what to say except maybe the next type of story will. This next ghost story is called a jump story. Jump stories have a line that is repeated throughout the story. Each time the line is said with a scarier voice until the final time, when the line is yelled out loudly so that everyone "jumps" with fear. This classic example, again from *The Kids Campfire Book*, is Mark Twain's story, "The Golden Arm."

A man and a woman who used to live near here, were in a car accident. The woman lost her arm. The husband felt so guilty that he bought his wife a golden arm.

Soon the man began to think of all the things he could buy with the gold in the arm and plotted to kill his wife. But, strangely enough, she died of natural causes before he could carry out his plan. He stole her golden arm from the coffin before she was buried.

The first night after her funeral, he was lying in bed when he thought he heard a voice moaning in the wind outside. "Where is my golden arm?"

He told himself he must be hearing things and soon fell asleep.

The next night, about midnight, he heard a moaning just outside the front door. "Where is my golden arm?"

It took a little longer before he fell asleep.

The third night, the man locked the front door and pushed a chair under the door knob. He fell asleep but around midnight he heard a moaning that seemed to come from right outside his bedroom door. This time he thought it was his wife's voice. "Where is my golden arm?"

The next night, he locked the front door and pushed the couch in front of it. He locked his bedroom door and pushed the chest of drawers in front of it too. In the middle of the night he woke up to a moaning that seemed to come from beside his bed. This time, he was sure it was his wife's voice. "Where is my golden arm?"

Now turn and look at your one listener and shout—"*You've got it!*"

Having a few of these classics in your storytelling back pocket is a good start, but sometimes it can be even more fun to create your own story. The following is a list of things to include in your story to really grab your readers. I say "you" in the following list, but it also can be a made-up character.

- Think of a good setting. For example, try an insane asylum, a haunted church, your middle school, or a haunted telephone booth.

- Think of a good "what if" that makes the situation scary. For example, what if you are trapped in the haunted basement of your school.

- Brainstorm all of the scary things that could happen, such as noises, lights turning off and on, strange smells, etc.

- How did you end up in this scary situation?

- What is going to happen? And what problem do you need to face?

- How are you going to get out or resolve the scary problem?

- Make up a scary and surprising ending that might shock your audience.

One thing that can help fuel your writing is if you've had a ghostly experience in the past. Knowing how you felt when you saw something that you couldn't quite explain makes it easier to imagine how your listener is feeling. Here are some examples of ghost sightings from some kids that I know.

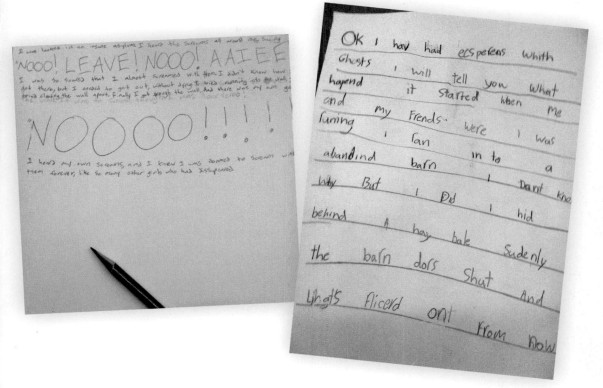

So get out your pen and paper and start to write that creepy tale that has been forming in your head. Aim to hold everyone's attention at the next sleepover or campfire with your creative powers. And if you get stuck, look through some of the haunted house stories in this book and use those to get you rolling. I know you will scare the pants off people!

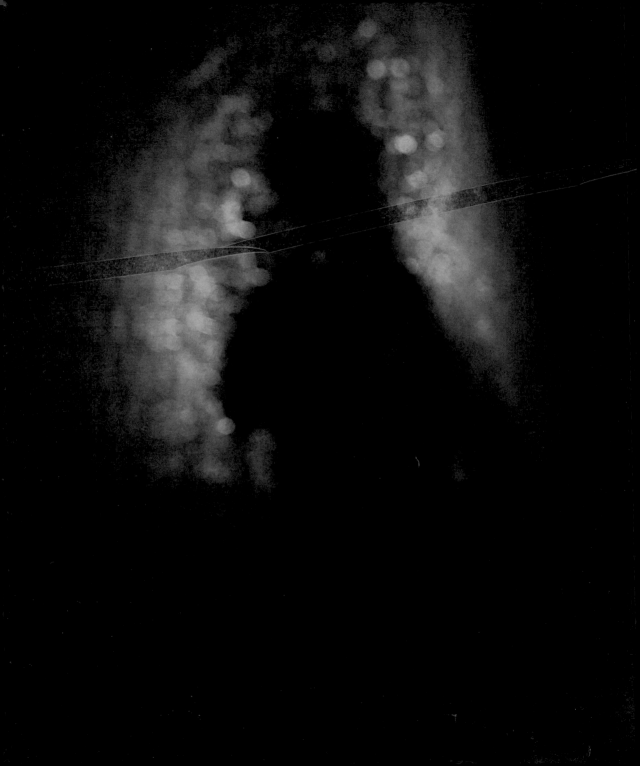

CHAPTER 6
CONCLUSION

If you have made it to this point, congratulations! I think you have what it takes to look a ghost in the eye, or whatever part of it might appear, and take some good notes about the experience. I think you have the tools to hear footsteps and check if anyone is really home before assuming it is a ghost.

As you begin this pursuit, remember that this hobby is about asking questions just like many of the best hobbies are. You are setting out to answer one of the oldest questions in human history: Is there really such a thing as a ghost? If so, how do you know and how can you prove it? If there aren't ghosts, how can you prove that? And how can you really know any of it for sure?

Ghost hunting not only gives a lot of good goosebumps, but it can unite you with others in the search of the unknown. You can share experiences with your gift of storytelling. You can help solve mysteries together. But along the road there will certainly be bumps and scares, and maybe even a bruised knee or two. There will be boring investigations where nothing will happen, and lots and lots of photos that don't turn up a single spectral sight. People who say they have ghosts in their house might just have a window that lets in a breeze, which makes a door swing. At these points you can throw up your hands and give up or you can keep searching and continue to ask the questions. I hope you are one of the ones who keep asking. I hope you are one of the ones whose flashlight will continue to shine in the darkness and open minds. And always remember the wise words of Lori Summers, who says, "There's no magical secret code for ghost hunters, no ancient mantra that will let you conjure up spirits at will and see them whenever you like. A ghost hunter is primarily a scientific investigator, and that's how you should think of yourself, as a scientist. A good scientist is objective and thorough."

GHOSTLY ENCOUNTER

Record your sightings on the following pages!

GHOST HUNTER'S NOTEBOOK

Sighting date:

Time:

Location:

Temperature:

Strange noises and phenomena observed:

Ghost appearance:

Ghostly communication:

GHOST HUNTER'S NOTEBOOK

Sighting date:

Time:

Location:

Temperature:

Strange noises and phenomena observed:

Ghost appearance:

Ghostly communication:

GHOST HUNTER'S NOTEBOOK

Sighting date:

Time:

Location:

Temperature:

Strange noises and phenomena observed:

Ghost appearance:

Ghostly communication:

GHOST HUNTER'S NOTEBOOK

Sighting date:

Time:

Location:

Temperature:

Strange noises and phenomena observed:

Ghost appearance:

Ghostly communication:

RESOURCES

Ghost Hunting: True Stories of Unexplained Phenomena from the Atlantic Paranormal Society by Jason Hawes and Grant Wilson

Ghosts? The Evidence and the Arguments: Usborne Paranormal Guides by Gillian Doherty

Ghosts and the Supernatural by Colin Wilson

Ghosts and Real-Life Ghost Hunters by Michael Teitelbaum

Tales of Real Haunting by Tony Allan

The Everything Guide to Ghost Hunting: Tips, Tools, and Techniques for Exploring the Supernatural World by Melissa Martin Ellis

The Ghost Hunter's Handbook: A Field Guide to the Paranormal by Lori Summers

The Usborne Book of Ghosts and Hauntings by Anna Claybourne

Whose Haunting the White House: The Presidents Mansion and the Ghosts Who Live There by Jeff Belanger and illustrated by Rick Powell

Lost Loot: Ghostly New England Treasure Tales by Patricia Hughes

Ghost Trackers: The Unreal World of Ghosts, Ghost Hunting and the Paranormal by Chris Gutcheon

The Kids Campfire Book by Ann Love and Jane Drake

Ghosthunting101.comsyfy.com/ghosthuntersghoststop.com

ACKNOWLEDGMENTS

Writing can be spooky. Sometimes there are dark pathways and unexplained losses of time. Sometimes you even hear voices. But having so many amazing people to help light the way makes it all seem doable and a lot less scary.

I want to thank my editor, Michael Steere, for never getting spooked, even when deadlines are tight and files get filled with strange poltergeists. A big thank you goes to Lynda Chilton, the Harry Houdini of designers, for weaving her magic once again. Thanks to the incredible team at Globe Pequot who help my books find the light of day: Jim Childs, Margaret Milnes, Sharon Kunz, Shana Capozza, Jessica Nelligan, Stephanie Scott, Amy Alexander, and Dennis Hayes.

And thank you to all the brave and inquisitive ghost hunters that I interviewed: K and L Soul Catchers, Karen Curtis and Lee Bisson; Jamie Dube; Kenneth Ort; Bryanna Dube; and Jake Drake.

Thank you to the Rockport Library for always letting me test out my ideas. Thank you to Bennett, Piper, Finn, Cooper, and Tessa for sharing your scary stories and creativity with me.

But the biggest thanks of all go to my family, Jeff, Phoebe, and Daphne, who are always willing to investigate the bumps in the night and who make everything into one grand adventure.